Grandmother's Recipe Journal

Grandmother's Recipe Journal

Bluestreak
an imprint of Weldon Owen International
PO Box 3088, San Rafael, CA 94912
www.weldonowen.com

Printed in China

ISBN-13: 978-1-68188-827-9

10 9 8 7 6 5 4 3 2 1

Introduction

A Private Note to Grandkids from the Publisher

We're going to print this note really small, so your grandma can't read it. It's private, only for you.

You may have childhood memories of holiday meals, Sunday dinners, and freshly baked treats, but have you ever thought about how your grandmother makes your family's classic dishes? What is her best-kept kitchen secret? What is her specialty dish? What is her advice for cooking with confidence? How did she learn to cook? What were your grandma's favorite — and least favorite — foods to eat as a child?

This journal is her place to share with you the recipes and culinary memories that you will want to know one day, even if you don't realize it yet.

And as you grow up, you will treasure this special keepsake, in which your grandmother has shared her beloved meals, memories, and wisdom—just for you! So even if it seems like a weird gift now, hold onto it, talk to your grandmother about it, ask her to tell you more of her prized recipes, and one day you will be very happy that you did!

MY FAVORITE "SECRET" INGREDIENT I LIKE TO USE

RECIPE

SERVES:

INGREDIENTS

INSTRUCTIONS

"Grandma, he had often wanted to say, Is this where the world began? For surely it had begun in no other than a place like this. The kitchen, without doubt, was the center of creation, all things revolved about it; it was the pediment that sustained the temple."

—RAY BRADBURY

GRANDMA'S RECIPE FOR HAPPINESS

RECIPE

SERVES:

INGREDIENTS

INSTRUCTIONS

A DISH TO MAKE IF YOU DON'T HAVE A LOT OF TIME

RECIPE

SERVES:

INGREDIENTS

INSTRUCTIONS

"There is no love sincerer than the love of food."

—GEORGE BERNARD SHAW

SOME OF OUR FAMILY FAVORITES INCLUDE

RECIPE

SERVES:

INGREDIENTS

INSTRUCTIONS

INGREDIENTS TO ALWAYS KEEP IN YOUR KITCHEN

RECIPE

SERVES:

INGREDIENTS

INSTRUCTIONS

“A man who is stingy with saffron is capable of seducing his own grandmother.”

—NORMAN DOUGLAS

A RECIPE FROM MY CHILDHOOD

RECIPE

SERVES:

INGREDIENTS

INSTRUCTIONS

MY BEST BAKING TIP

RECIPE

SERVES:

INGREDIENTS

INSTRUCTIONS

"I'm pretty sure that eating chocolate keeps wrinkles away because I have never seen a ten-year-old with a Hershey bar and crows feet."

—AMY NEFTZGER

TRADITIONAL FAMILY DISHES THAT WE ATE

RECIPE

SERVES:

INGREDIENTS

INSTRUCTIONS

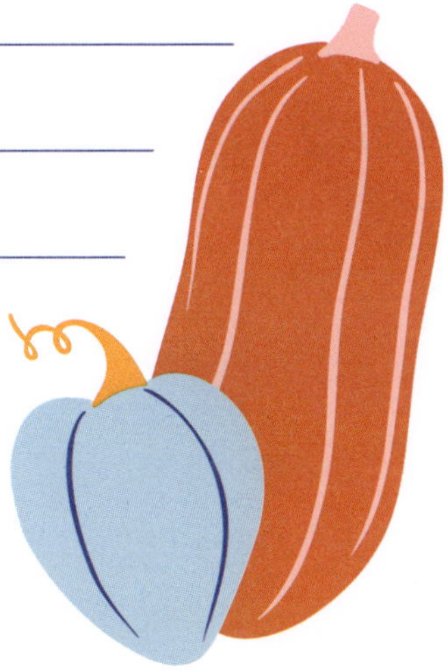

THE BEST COOKING SKILL TO LEARN

RECIPE

SERVES:

INGREDIENTS

INSTRUCTIONS

"The only real stumbling block is fear of failure.
In cooking you've got to have a what-the-hell attitude."

—JULIA CHILD

WHAT WE TALKED ABOUT AT THE DINNER TABLE

RECIPE

SERVES:

INGREDIENTS

INSTRUCTIONS

MY FAVORITE KITCHEN APPLIANCE TO HAVE AROUND

RECIPE

SERVES:

INGREDIENTS

INSTRUCTIONS

"Teaching kids how to feed themselves and how to live in a community responsibly is the center of an education."

—ALICE WATERS

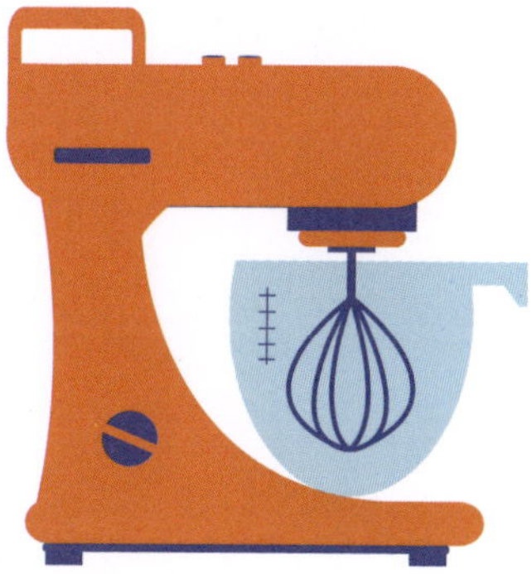

A MEMORY ABOUT FAMILY MEALS WHEN I WAS GROWING UP

RECIPE

SERVES:

INGREDIENTS

INSTRUCTIONS

MY FAVORITE COOKBOOK

RECIPE

SERVES:

INGREDIENTS

INSTRUCTIONS

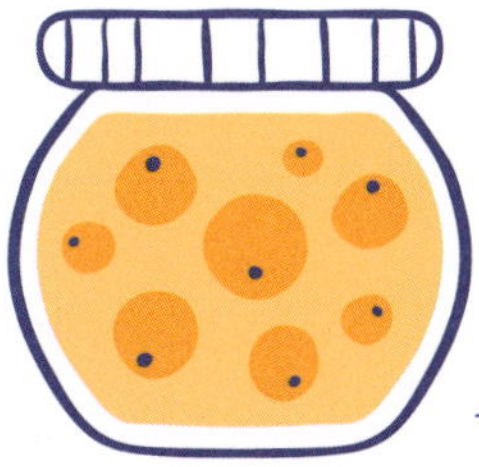

"Good food is very often, even most often, simple food."

—ANTHONY BOURDAIN

MY FAMILY'S RULES ABOUT DINNERTIME

RECIPE

SERVES:

INGREDIENTS

INSTRUCTIONS

SOMETHING THAT'S BETTER STORE-BOUGHT THAN HOMEMADE

RECIPE

SERVES:

INGREDIENTS

INSTRUCTIONS

"I come from a home where gravy is a beverage."

—ERMA BOMBECK

A RECIPE I GOT FROM MY MOTHER OR ANOTHER RELATIVE

RECIPE

SERVES:

INGREDIENTS

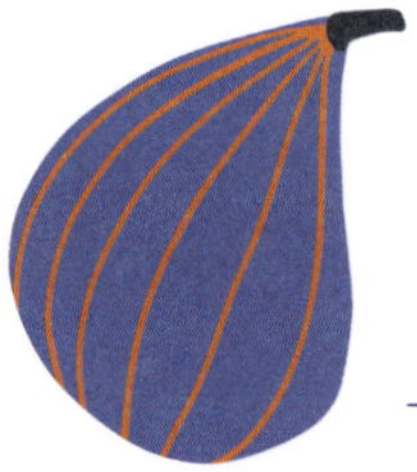

INSTRUCTIONS

A DISH THAT'S WORTH THE TIME IT TAKES TO PREPARE

RECIPE

SERVES:

INGREDIENTS

INSTRUCTIONS

"Don't eat anything your great-grandmother wouldn't recognize as food."

—MICHAEL POLLAN

MY FAVORITE FOODS AS A CHILD

RECIPE

SERVES:

INGREDIENTS

INSTRUCTIONS

THE MOST USEFUL KITCHEN UTENSIL

RECIPE

SERVES:

INGREDIENTS

INSTRUCTIONS

"Becoming a grandmother is wonderful.
One moment you're just a mother.
The next, you are all-wise and prehistoric."

—PAM BROWN

A FOOD I REALLY DID NOT LIKE AS A CHILD

RECIPE

SERVES:

INGREDIENTS

INSTRUCTIONS

A BASIC DISH WORTH MASTERING

RECIPE

SERVES:

INGREDIENTS

INSTRUCTIONS

"Cooking is at once child's play and adult joy. And cooking done with care is an act of love."

—CRAIG CLAIBORNE

THE BEST COOK IN MY FAMILY IS/WAS

RECIPE

SERVES:

INGREDIENTS

INSTRUCTIONS

A DISH THAT TASTES BETTER THE NEXT DAY

RECIPE

SERVES:

INGREDIENTS

INSTRUCTIONS

“Pull up a chair. Take a taste. Come join us.
Life is so endlessly delicious.”

—RUTH REICHL

SOME DISHES WE ATE ON SPECIAL OCCASIONS

RECIPE

SERVES:

INGREDIENTS

INSTRUCTIONS

IF MY KITCHEN HAD ONE RULE, IT WOULD BE

RECIPE

SERVES:

INGREDIENTS

INSTRUCTIONS

"Behind every *Guide Michelin* chef there was a woman, usually a four-foot cataract-ridden old granny from whom he'd filched his best recipes."

—KAREN KARBO

MEALS MY MOTHER OR FATHER LOVED TO MAKE

RECIPE

SERVES:

INGREDIENTS

INSTRUCTIONS

THE BEST SIDE DISH

RECIPE

SERVES:

INGREDIENTS

INSTRUCTIONS

"Grandparents enjoy most the company of
their grandchildren. For with them,
they experience the miracle of being ten again."

—MEETA AHLUWALIA

MY FAVORITE MEMORY IN THE KITCHEN

RECIPE

SERVES:

INGREDIENTS

INSTRUCTIONS

THE BEST DISH TO MAKE FOR SOMEONE ELSE

RECIPE

SERVES:

INGREDIENTS

INSTRUCTIONS

"After a good dinner one can forgive anybody, even one's own relations."

—OSCAR WILDE

FAVORITE RECIPES MY GRANDMOTHER MADE

RECIPE

SERVES:

INGREDIENTS

INSTRUCTIONS

A GOOD DISH TO MAKE ON A COLD DAY

RECIPE

SERVES:

INGREDIENTS

INSTRUCTIONS

"You are the sun, Grandma,
you are the sun in my life."

—KITTY TSUI

SOME OF THE FOODS MY FAMILY LIKED TO EAT

RECIPE

SERVES:

INGREDIENTS

INSTRUCTIONS

A FOOD YOU SHOULD ALWAYS HAVE ON HAND FOR GUESTS

RECIPE

SERVES:

INGREDIENTS

INSTRUCTIONS

"On my day off, I rarely want to eat restaurant food unless I'm looking for new ideas or recipes to steal. What I want to eat is home cooking, somebody's—anybody's—mother's or grandmother's food."

—ANTHONY BOURDAIN

WHAT WE ATE ON OUR WEDDING DAY

RECIPE

SERVES:

INGREDIENTS

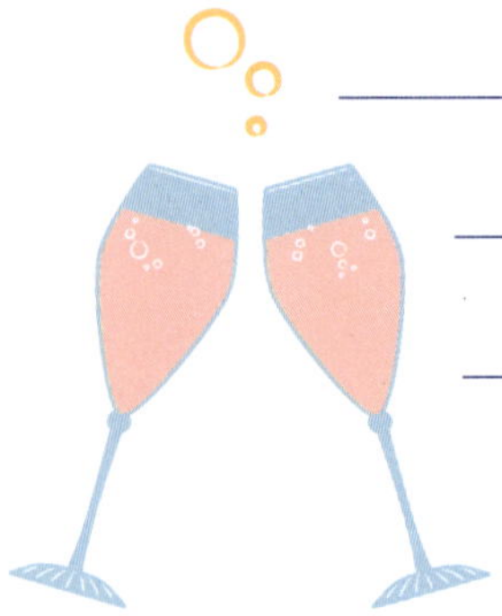

INSTRUCTIONS

THE BIGGEST LESSON I'VE LEARNED AS A COOK

RECIPE

SERVES:

INGREDIENTS

INSTRUCTIONS

"All you need is love. But a little chocolate now and then doesn't hurt."

—CHARLES M. SCHULZ

THE DISH I MADE MOST OFTEN

RECIPE

SERVES:

INGREDIENTS

INSTRUCTIONS

A CULINARY TIP MY MOTHER PASSED DOWN TO ME

RECIPE

SERVES:

INGREDIENTS

INSTRUCTIONS

"My grandmother started walking five miles a day when she was sixty. She's ninety-seven now, and we don't know where the heck she is."

—ELLEN DEGENERES

A RECIPE FROM YOUR PARENT'S CHILDHOOD

RECIPE

SERVES:

INGREDIENTS

INSTRUCTIONS

MY SPECIALTY DISH

RECIPE

SERVES:

INGREDIENTS

INSTRUCTIONS

"I sustain myself with the love of family."

—Maya Angelou

ONE RECIPE I WOULD LIKE TO TEACH YOU

RECIPE

SERVES:

INGREDIENTS

INSTRUCTIONS

ONE OF MY FAVORITE DISHES NOW

RECIPE

SERVES:

INGREDIENTS

INSTRUCTIONS

"Seize the moment. Remember all those women on the *Titanic* who waved off the dessert cart."

—ERMA BOMBECK

A FOOD I'VE ALWAYS WANTED TO TRY

RECIPE

SERVES:

INGREDIENTS

INSTRUCTIONS

SOME WORDS OF WISDOM WHEN A RECIPE GOES AWRY

RECIPE

SERVES:

INGREDIENTS

INSTRUCTIONS

“My grandmother is over eighty and still doesn’t need glasses. Drinks right out of the bottle.”

—HENRY YOUNGMAN

A MEAL I WISH I COULD HAVE AGAIN

RECIPE

SERVES:

INGREDIENTS

INSTRUCTIONS

A DISH THAT SMELLS NOSTALGIC TO ME

RECIPE

SERVES:

INGREDIENTS

INSTRUCTIONS

"Young people need something stable to hang on to—a culture connection, a sense of their own past, a hope for their own future. Most of all, they need what grandparents can give them."

—JAY KESLER

Message to You

Here is a message from me to you, with all my love and wisdom.